GOOD EGG

Dorothy Fortenberry

GW00683526

BROADWAY PLAY PUBLISHING INC
224 E 62nd St, NY, NY 10065
www.broadwayplaypub.com
info@broadwayplaypub.com

First printing July 2011
I S B N: 978-0-88145-495-6

Book design: Marie Donovan
Page make-up: Adobe Indesign
Typeface: Palatino
Printed and bound in the U S A

The world premiere of GOOD EGG was produced
by The Red Fern Theater Company (Melanie
Moyer Williams, Executive Artistic Director). The
first performance was on 21 October 2010 with the
following cast and creative contributors:

MEG .... Andrea Day
MATT ....Dan McCabe

Director ....Kel Haney
Sound designer .... Katherine A Buechner
Lighting designer ....Chuan-Chi Chan
Costume designer .... Katherine Akiko Day
Scenic designer ....Scott Dougan
Choreographer ....Karl Maier
Composer .... Colin Wambsgans
Production stage manager ....Michal V Mendelson
Prop master/Ass't director ....Megan Eileen Kosmoski
Rehearsal S M/Puppet designer .... Kate Pressman
Publicist .... Katie Rosin/Kampfire P R

CHARACTERS & SETTING

MEG, *28*
MATT, *23, her brother*
Time: Early spring, present day
Place: Washington, DC

Scene 1

(The inside of MEG's *womb)*

MEG: This is my womb. Welcome, really. I'm happy
to be showing you around. I'm not usually a bragger,
but—come on. Pink. Healthy-looking. Spacious...
Those of you in the back, you're closer to the Fallopian
tubes, so I hope your view's not obstructed, but, I think
no matter where you are, you get a sense, right? The
possibilities. I wanted to take this opportunity now
to orient you a bit, before Adrianna, my gynecologist,
shows up with her jellied speculum. To give some
context. I love context. So, hysteria. Aaaaaaaah!
Just kidding. I'm actually a very calm, well-
organized—. Hysteria is an ancient disease first
described by Hippocrates, in which a woman's
hystera—her—
(She gestures around her.)
—when not otherwise occupied by a child, would
go wandering around her body, looking for babies
to house. It's kind of sweet, really, this intrepid
organ, unsatisfied with its lonely life, goes in search
of something better. So it ends up in the stomach or
maybe the heart, hoping to find the beginnings of a
child. It's an immigrant story, really.
Fast forward to medieval times, and hysteria's still
around, being diagnosed in virgins, widows, nuns
...See a pattern? All the way up to the nineteenth
century, which was a high point—or, I guess, a low
one. Tons of ladies in corsets going batty, for which,

and I am not making this up, I'm a Congressional
researcher, doctors invented the vibrator. Maybe
you've heard about this? Real deal, big ol' electric
models or some with water jets. Saved them the trouble
of treating their patients manually. Years before
you could buy an electric vacuum cleaner or an iron
...And, okay, slight digression here, I realize that the
traditional feminist perspective is that vast numbers of
women were misdiagnosed because the male medical
establishment feared their latent power or whatever,
but I'm just saying ...Look. It's 1870-something, there's
no sex shops, there's no Internet, the only way the
ladies were going to get their hands—etc—on this
machinery was with a hysteria diagnosis. So they'd cry
a little, break a few dishes. Wouldn't you?

After this comes Freud who attributes the whole thing
to psychoneurosis caused by repressed memories,
but the diagnosis dwindles as the twentieth century
goes on. In 1980, the American Psychiatric Association
removed the word "hysteria" from their manual, and
now people get diagnosed with "panic attacks" or
"fibromyalgia" and put on antidepressants instead of
sex toys. Progress.

And. Now that we have our context...I got diagnosed
a few months ago with this disease of the womb called
endometriosis. That's, uh, why I'm here, waiting for
my exam. Don't worry, it's not contagious, you should
all be fine. Although, actually, be on the lookout for
floating pieces of—. It's this disease where tissue from
the lining of the uterus gets found in other parts of the
body. Sometimes near the ovaries, sometimes near the
bladder. In my case, they found it behind the uterus—
over that way—in what's known as the cul-de-sac.
Seriously. I don't even like driving in cul-de-sacs.

And, um, when Adrianna told me what was going
on, why my periods hurt so much, I kind of lost it. I

mean, it's my womb roaming around my body, right? Technically, twenty-first-century-wise, that's what's happening. You know who's most likely to get it, too? Women who've never had children—back to the virgins, widows, nuns... In my case, the tissue didn't have to travel too far, but I've read about women who have it in their arms, their lungs. This one woman, no kidding, gets really heavy nosebleeds every twenty-eight days. Oh, and one of endometriosis's big side effects? Infertility. I know. Bits of my body are flaking off to look for a baby and despite a lifetime of good behavior, I'm hysterical.

Scene 2

(MEG *and* MATT's *apartment. She has returned from the gynecologist's, and they are watching* Singin' in the Rain *on television and eating popcorn.*)

MEG: Ta da.

MATT: You have got to be kidding.

MEG: What?

MATT: I cancelled my date with Christy because you said I had to come to home. You texted me S-I-T-R, exclamation point.

MEG: Singin'. In. The. Rain.

MATT: That's not like an abbreviation normal people use.

MEG: Look, I was just casually flipping channels and— lo! Behold! It's an omen.

MATT: *(Affectionately)* You're a bitch. An obsessive, controlling—

MEG: I have good luck. The universe provides for siblings. Shhh—here it comes.

MATT: Wait, this is a D V D.

MEG: Get ready. *(Along with the movie)* "Yes, yes, yes." *(Hits his leg)* Go.

MATT: *(Grudgingly)* "No, no, no."

MEG: "Yes, yes, yes."

MATT: "No, no, no."

(MATT hits MEG with a piece of popcorn.)

MEG: Stop that.

MATT: Admit it. You want something.

MEG: I want to hang out with you.

MATT: Salt and sugar popcorn? Did you make the cocoa too?

MEG: It was easy.

(MATT grabs MEG and noogies her hair)

MATT: Tell me what's up.

MEG: Ow, stop it! Nothing's up. Jeez.

(MEG shoves MATT off, and rearranges her hair.)

MATT: Then why are you making me watch Singin' in the Rain on a Friday night like we're little kids?

MEG: I just want to have a nice time with you.

MATT: You know, you could invite some real seven year-olds if you wanted. Hang out in elementary school parking lots, scoop 'em up in your van.

MEG: I don't have a van. I have a Jetta.

MATT: Meg.

MEG: They're going to sing "Good Morning" soon, with the eye-cover-dancey thing. "Good morning, good morning." *(She demonstrates with her sleeves)* Come on, sit next to me. Snack.

MATT: If you're going to treat me like a child, I've got no choice but to behave like one.

(MATT *straddles* MEG's *head.*)

MEG: Oh my God, don't even, what are you—ow—

MATT: If you don't tell me what's going on, I'm going to have to fart on your head.

MEG: Matt, you little—

MATT: It's not going to be pleasant. Just to warn you. I'm feeling like this one's particularly stenchy.

MEG: Get off. I can't see movie—

MATT: Five, four, three, two, one—

MEG: I'm going to have a baby. *(Pause)* Matt!

MATT: I'm sorry. I was surprised. It slipped out.

MEG: Ugh. *(She turns off the T V.)*

MATT: Really?

MEG: Yeah. I think so.

MATT: Oh my God. Are you—? Right now?

(MATT *touches* MEG's *stomach. She moves his hand away.*)

MEG: No, no. It's not that easy. It's not going to be that easy, but I went to see Adrianna today—my gynecologist—she said I can start gearing up, and, pretty soon, if it all goes well—

MATT: What are you talking about?

MEG: The thing I have—the endometriosis?

MATT: *(Silly voice)* Endometriosis?

MEG: The underwear drying in the shower once a month—

MATT: Yeah, what about it? Gross, by the way.

MEG: It makes it hard—my uterus is, like, fragile—so I need to plan more, but I think—

MATT: Planning with who? Who are you even dating?

MEG: I'm not. I'm using a donor.

MATT: Like a sperm donor? You recreated the movie musical afternoons of our childhood to tell me you're using a sperm donor?

MEG: Yeah, well, a kidney wouldn't really be much help.

MATT: Who is it? Where'd you meet him? Is it, like, some gay friend of yours? It's not Eliot.

MEG: No, I found him on the Internet.

MATT: Oh, awesome.

MEG: It is. He's definitely one of the best available. I mean, he's great. He plays the cello. And rows. As a hobby. He has hobbies.

MATT: Sounds like a bum.

MEG: You're judging?

MATT: A preppy bum.

MEG: He's really focused. He did the Peace Corps.

MATT: Yeah right.

MEG: He did.

MATT: On the Internet. Everyone says they did the Peace Corps on those things.

MEG: No they don't. How would you know?

MATT: Because I said I did the Peace Corps on nerve. com

MEG: Shut up. Where?

MATT: Madagascar.

MEG: Yeah? How was it?

MATT: Really meaningful, thanks. Life-changing. I still keep in touch with Mtumbo, my little African brother.

MEG: I can't believe you.

MATT: You're really going to do this?

MEG: Yeah.

MATT: Why?

MEG: Um, because I want a baby, and I know it's harder this way, but—. I thought you'd be happy for me.

MATT: I am, sure, but—

MEG: Good. You're going to be its uncle. That's fun.

MATT: Okay.

MEG: Come on, be happy. You're the first person I told.

MATT: After Adrianna the gynecologist.

MEG: I couldn't really do it without her.

MATT: Well, you could. I don't know if you know this, I think maybe Dad forgot to give you the talk, but when a man and woman love each other—

MEG: Matt.

MATT: Fine. I'm sorry. This is a celebration. Whee.

MEG: Thank you.

MATT: So, where's this guy from? Mister Sperminator.

MEG: Virginia.

MATT: You got Republican sperm?

MEG: No, Jesus. You think I didn't check for that? He's a Democrat.

MATT: Virginia?

MEG: It's a blue state. Ish.

MATT: Is it here?

MEG: What?

MATT: The sperm, is it like in a Dixie cup in the fridge or something because I don't want to—

MEG: No, no. It's at the lab.

MATT: Okay, cool, just checking. And when—

MEG: In about a month, probably. I'll start the shots tonight.

MATT: Like shot-shots?

MEG: Small needle. I need to go through a cycle on Clomid so they can get some eggs, and—

MATT: Meg, who is this guy?

MEG: He's genetically perfect. A-plus. I'll show you the chart.

MATT: Yeah, no thanks. I mean, what does he look like, is the baby at least going to be hot?

MEG: I'm not sure, exactly.

MATT: Because, I gotta say, based on what you're contributing, this bugger could use some hot D N A.

(MEG *throws a fistful of popcorn at* MATT.)

MATT: So he's not hot.

MEG: They don't let you see a picture or anything because it's anonymous. So you can't track the guy down and demand child support or invite him to birthday parties or whatever.

MATT: But you still know what he looks like, right? Come on, that's got to be like first on the profile.

MEG: Actually, in this market, it's education level. He's getting a PhD, did I tell you? Had to pay extra, but—

MATT: And yet he still has time to play the cello and row. What a guy.

MEG: I don't know what he looks like exactly. He's tall. Six foot. Blue eyes. Brown hair. Not balding, they ask that. Freckles.

MATT: Meg.

MEG: What?

MATT: He looks like Dad.

MEG: No, he doesn't.

MATT: But your description. That could be Dad.

MEG: Yeah, or I mean, it was pretty generic. You could go out on the street tomorrow and find like a hundred people getting off the Metro at Farragut North who fit that description. Six foot. Blue eyes. Brown hair. Freckles. It's no big deal.

MATT: He looks like Dad.

MEG: Whatever.

MATT: Meg, he looks like me.

MEG: He's not. He's not anything like you. Or Dad.

MATT: I didn't mean it as an insult.

(Pause)

MEG: Right. Of course—. I didn't—.

MATT: I know.

MEG: I just—. I think it's going to be really fun. This kid. For both of us. Come on, how much fun would it be to share this with a little, cute, soft person?

MATT: This?

MEG: This. *(She turns on the T V)*

MEG: We can hang out and snuggle and watch all the musicals we want. We can play dress-up and re-enact the big production numbers.

MATT: That's what we'll do for fun? Have you met any actual kids recently? All they care about is, like, vampires.

MEG: It's perfect. We were always short one in the three-person scenes, anyway.

MATT: You've got it all planned out, huh?

MEG: Be happy for me. Please. This is a big deal.

MATT: I know. I am happy, but, Meg, have you thought about what this is going to mean? A baby?

MEG: Yes. We can get it little, tiny tap shoes.

MATT: I'm serious. It's expensive and demanding.

MEG: I'm serious, too. I've done the research: I've been taking prenatal vitamins and I stopped eating tuna and I'm cutting out coffee and luncheon meats and—

MATT: But—

MEG: I can afford it, don't worry, I'll spend my money from selling the house.

MATT: I'm just concerned a little, that, like, there's stuff—

MEG: I've got it under control.

MATT: Meg—

MEG: *(Watching T V)* Shut up, shut up. This is the best part.

(The song Good Morning *from* Singin' in the Rain *plays.)*

Scene 3

(Back in the womb. Four weeks later.)

MEG: Egg. Meg. Meg. Egg.
Ever since I went on the hormones last month, I've
been having these dreams about the Anne Geddes
babies. You know those photographs of the babies
in the felt vegetable costumes, like eggplant baby or
whatever.

*(Behind her, a projection of an Anne Geddes photograph
appears.)*

MEG: It's meant to be cute, but it's also a little bizarre.
It's like baby carrot, you know, or baby zucchini, like
on a tray, next to dip, only it's an actual baby carrot
because it's a baby wearing a carrot hat. Why does a
person take these photographs? What possesses you to
want to adorn infants with vegetal felt? Aren't babies
cute enough on their own? I mean, when you look at a
baby, do you think "Oh, you're all right, but you'd be
adorable as a turnip." No, you just think "Wow. Baby."
So why does Anne Geddes put them in the costumes?
And why am I dreaming about this literal cabbage
patch?
But of course. My eggs are going to be harvested. No
wonder I'm dreaming of produce.
The harvest's today, actually, that's why we're back.
Maybe I should have worn gingham. It's going to go
great, Adrianna does this all the time. Just remove the
eggs from whenever they've all ovulated themselves
to, put 'em in a jar, and insert the trusty sperm. She
does it all nice and safe inside some glass containers
in the lab—in vitro, as they say—and then, in a couple
days, I'll get one of the eggs back. I'll be sowing the
seeds to make my own crop. Planting time. Right here.
Meg. Egg. Egg. Meg.

Scene 4

(MEG *and* MATT's *apartment, the night following the egg harvest. It's messier than it was last time. He is working on wiring a Speak & Spell toy. She enters, coming home from work and the gynecologist's, carrying the mail.*)

MEG: Did you—? Have a pizza party?

MATT: What, you don't like it?

MEG: No, it's great. How I always pictured this room.

MATT: Good.

(MEG *surveys the living room chaos, picks up* MATT's *jacket and folds it on the back of a chair.*)

MEG: Did you call Eliot's friend?

MATT: Did I call him? No, I'll send him an e-mail tomorrow. That way I can attach a resume or whatever.

MEG: I told him you'd call.

MATT: You can call him and tell him that I'll be sending him an e-mail.

MEG: (*Looking at the Speak & Spell*) Did you fix that yet?

MATT: It's not broken.

MEG: Right.

MATT: Bumper crop? At the harvest?

MEG: Blue ribbon in the state fair. You know, you think they only award it to the biggest eggs, but actually—

MATT: Then it's standardized testing next, right? For your little Meglets?

MEG: Hm?

MATT: The Egg-lets?

MEG: Yeah. Tomorrow, like I said.

MATT: How do you think they're going to do? Have they been studying enough? Are they good testers? That's what the teachers would always say, "Are you sure you're Meg's brother? She was always such a good tester." I bet your babies will—

MEG: They're not babies.

MATT: No, I'm rooting for them. Really.

MEG: They're cells. *(She starts to pack up the spare toy parts)*

MATT: Hey, what are you doing?

MEG: It's a mess.

MATT: It's a project.

MEG: A clump of eight cells. That's all. With the potential—

MATT: Right, the potential—

MEG: To become a person. *(She starts to coil cable)*

MATT: I'm going to use that cable.

MEG: For what? *(She waits for a response)* I'm getting a burrito. *(She starts to leave)*

MATT: I've been researching those tests.

(MEG stops.)

MATT: I mean, I know it's your thing and all, but Google's pretty dope, and I found out lots of stuff last night.

MEG: When?

MATT: Couldn't sleep.

MEG: Are you doing okay?

MATT: I'm fine. You don't just get those tests, one doesn't. You have to ask.

MEG: I'm a high-risk patient, because of the endometriosis, it made sense to—

MATT: You had to ask. To request it.

MEG: Fine, yes.

MATT: To screen your embryos before they're implanted in your uterus.

MEG: It's a really routine procedure, I told you, it's done all the time in cases like this. To look for disease, abnormality, to make sure the baby's healthy and normal and—

MATT: Not bipolar.

(Pause)

MEG: Matt. Mattie.

MATT: You didn't think I'd find out? You said they were checking for diseases—

MEG: And they are. For Huntington's and Parkinson's and Alzheimer's and M S and—

MATT: Me?

MEG: It's a new test. They just located the genes recently, and—

MATT: You're taking advantage of the technology. It's on the Metropolitan Fertility website for Christ's sake. Like "New! Improved! Now with no bipolar!"

MEG: It doesn't say that—

MATT: You want to argue about the wording?

MEG: I didn't think it would make you this upset.

MATT: Which is why you didn't tell me, right?

MEG: It is a totally routine, common thing to do, just to be on the safe side. I like the safe side. That's all it is.

MATT: Um, no, it's rifling through a selection of babies—fine, fine of embryos—and then choosing your favorite, which is totally weird and gross and disgusting.

MEG: It didn't disgust you when I told you they were screening for Down Syndrome.

MATT: That's different.

MEG: How?

(MATT *doesn't know.*)

MEG: It's a precaution. Take an umbrella and it won't rain. Come on, you know me.

MATT: Yeah, and you're better than this.

MEG: Please don't make a big deal—

MATT: Don't be such a pussy.

MEG: A what?

MATT: It's not done yet, right? What if you took the risk? So maybe your kid would be born bipolar, so what? You'd deal with the shit that comes up.

MEG: Because it's easy? Dealing with you and your moods and your meds and your stuff—

MATT: Please, would you please just hear me out. Deal with it, if it happens, but don't throw away some little dude's life just because they might take a little more effort. You can do it. Look at you. You're, whatever, you're the superstar. You could be the mom to a bipolar kid.

MEG: I know I could, Matt. I just don't think I could be the mom to two bipolar kids. *(Pause)* I didn't mean it like that.

MATT: Yeah, I think you did.

MEG: I appreciate that you're thinking so much about this stuff, but it's really my decision, okay? And you don't have to like it, but I wish you could support me.

MATT: You want me to support you without liking what you're doing?

MEG: That's how I support you.

MATT: Um, no it isn't.

MEG: It's how I try to support you. Unconditionally.

MATT: That's what you've been aiming for?

MEG: You're going to be her uncle.

MATT: Her? Cause you can pick the gender, too, right?

MEG: I'm asking you nicely to be a part of our new family.

MATT: All the choices laid out in front of you like Baskin Robbins. All thirty-one flavors.

MEG: I don't have thirty-one embryos.

MATT: How many then?

MEG: Seven.

MATT: And you picked the girl?

MEG: They ask you to—

MATT: With or without rainbow sprinkles? Low-fat? No-fat?

MEG: It's not a joke.

MATT: You got a name picked out yet? Who am I kidding, of course you have a name picked out. You probably have a whole collection of name possibilities on pink note-cards somewhere, starting with A. Aaliyah? No. Abigail? Maybe.

MEG: I am having this kid alone and I need all the support I can get. Please.

(Pause)

MATT: Okay, fine. I'll support you, whatever that means.

MEG: Thank you.

MATT: You're going to name her after Mom, aren't you? *(Pause)* Katherine?

MEG: It's a good name.

MATT: Will you call her Kathy, like Mom? Or Kat?

MEG: Maybe. She can pick her own nickname, once she can talk.

MATT: You never went to therapy, did you? After Mom died. Someone, some guidance counselor or other made me go, but you slipped through the cracks, right? Just tested your way out of it.

MEG: You are being totally—

MATT: You never went to therapy?

MEG: I didn't need it, all right?

MATT: How did you ever make it past the screening process at Metropolitan Fert?

MEG: There is no screening process. There's a form. And an interview. I'm very good at interviews.

MATT: You're too much.

MEG: Anyway, since when are you pro-therapy?

(MATT gives MEG a look.)

MEG: I'm not, like, trying to recreate Mom, okay?

MATT: You said it, I didn't.

MEG: It's no big deal.

MATT: So name her something besides Katherine.

MEG: I don't want to.

MATT: Big deal.

MEG: You don't understand.

MATT: I understand way better than you want me to, and it's not going to work.

MEG: Um, that's super-supportive.

MATT: Not that. Sure, you'll probably get pregnant—you're good with concrete goals—but this whole thing? It won't work. It can't. It doesn't matter what you do, or how much you spend. You're not going to get your family back.

MEG: I don't want—

MATT: It's not going to be Version 2.0—with healthier offspring, better Christmas presents, and no death.

MEG: Great, thank you, thank you for the life lesson.

MATT: You're welcome.

MEG: Because as an unemployed hobbyist, you are in such an excellent position to tell other people how to live. This is none of your business.

MATT: You asked for my support.

MEG: Your support, not your bullshit amateur psychology.

MATT: And I have jobs, freelance design jobs. I'm actually working on a lot right now, which is why I was too busy to call Eliot's friend—

MEG: Uh huh.

MATT: Look, if you want me involved, then I'm going to be involved, and I think—

MEG: Mattie, I just want a child.

MATT: A perfect child.

MEG: A better child. That's all anyone wants, for their child to be a little bit better and a little bit happier than they are.

MATT: I really can't believe you didn't go to therapy after Mom died.

MEG: What was I going to talk about? She was dead. It wasn't a surprise or anything.

MATT: Still—

MEG: Besides, who was going to make me go? Dad? In those days?

MATT: He might have—

MEG: Come on.

MATT: He wasn't that bad. I don't remember him being that bad.

MEG: He was worse.

MATT: You're exaggerating.

MEG: You know how you got into therapy? I signed the form.

MATT: No you didn't. What, you forged—

MEG: Yes, I did. After you went to bed, I went through his mail, and all the notes you brought home from school, and I signed his signature so you could go to therapy. Or on the trip to the science museum, or to Fun Land or whatever.

MATT: If it's any consolation, the therapist sucked.

MEG: It's not.

MATT: So did Fun Land. Major misnomer.

MEG: I'm just saying—I know what our family was. And I'm not trying to repeat it.

MATT: Did you, like, balance his checkbook?

MEG: Sometimes.

MATT: You were fifteen. That's weird.

MEG: Yeah, well.

MATT: And you don't remember everything.

MEG: Okay.

MATT: Dad wasn't that bad all the time.

MEG: Bullshit.

MATT: I'm just saying, like when we were little, before Mom—, like when I was in kindergarten or whatever, he wasn't that bad.

MEG: Compared to what? Daytime television?

MATT: Compared to anybody. He was fun and exciting and took us on adventures—

MEG: Random car trips. Where we got lost and ran out of gas and—

MATT: Adventures. And he got us Chinese food whenever we wanted. And he made boring things interesting instead of the other way around like you do.

MEG: You just don't remember.

MATT: I do. He drove me to Lake Michigan once. In the middle of the night. Just me. I was, like, eight. You and Mom were asleep and he woke me up and said "Let's go" and we went and it was beautiful. The water was black and the sky was cloudy and cold. We stood on the Indiana sand dunes, they were covered in snow and we froze, but it was amazing. To get there, you know, from Bloomington, you have to go through Gary, which is bleak as shit, like Mordor or something, only it didn't look bleak then, or, if it did, it didn't matter. On the way there, at like midnight, he stopped at a Chinese restaurant and bought all their fortune cookies. They were my favorite part, always, of dinner, getting the fortune, and it was a surprise, he just pulled in and talked to the owner for a while and came out with this giant plastic bag of cookies. Just for me. Mom never did shit like that.

MEG: Why did he take you to Lake Michigan?

MATT: Meg, that's not the point. The point is it was the middle of the night and deserted and special.

MEG: Why wasn't he home? With us? What if something happened? If you were eight, Mom was already sick—

MATT: We came home. Like at five A M. We snuck in and he went into the bedroom with Mom and I went into my room and it was fine. God.

MEG: Maybe I shouldn't expect you to understand.

MATT: I understand—

MEG: If you think that's normal parenting—

MATT: Dad wasn't "normal," that's my whole—

MEG: Adrianna said if I want to have a kid, I need to do it soon, and so I am. Because I want to. Really, really badly.

MATT: Okay, okay, but having a kid doesn't necessarily mean doing it like this with the donor and the testing and, you could adopt—

MEG: No, I can't.

MATT: But—

MEG: I don't want to. The eggs are harvested. The embryos are made. This is my choice. I am choosing to have a child right now and I am choosing to conceive and not to adopt and I am choosing to test my embryos and I would really like you with me.

MATT: They weren't fun anymore.

MEG: Who?

MATT: The cookies. It's fun getting a fortune cookie at a Chinese restaurant because you don't know what it's going to be. If there are four people at dinner, you get four cookies, and you end up with the fortune you end up with and there's nothing you can do about it. When

Dad bought me the whole bag, he thought he was
being nice, and he was, it was this incredibly generous,
huge gesture, but it also turned out to be kind of
terrible. I spent the entire drive to Lake Michigan just
opening cookies and reading the fortunes, always
looking for something better. I ate the whole bag that
trip and I wasn't satisfied with a single cookie, and
when we got home, I put the fortunes in the trashcan,
and threw up in the sink.

MEG: My unborn child is not a cookie, Matt.

MATT: I'm just saying—when you can have everything
you want, sometimes you don't like anything you get.

Scene 5

*(Later that night. MATT finds MEG on the couch, eating a
microwaved burrito, and watching* Singin' in the Rain. *He
pops up behind her.)*

MATT: Moses supposes his toeses are roses.

MEG: But Moses supposes erroneously.

MATT: A Mose is Mose!

MEG: A rose is a rose.

MATT: A toes is a toes.

MEG: *(Simultaneous with* MATT *below)*
Hoop-de-doo-de-doo-doo.
Moses supposes his toeses are roses
But Moses supposes erroneously
Moses he knowes his toeses aren't roses
As Moses supposes his toeses to be.

MATT: *(Simultaneous with* MEG *above)*
Hoop-de-doo-de-doo-doo.
Moses supposes his toeses are roses
But Moses supposes erroneously

Moses he knowses his toeses aren't roses
As Moses supposes his toeses to be.

(MEG *turns off the T V*)

MATT: *(Still singing)* Moses...

MEG: Hey.

MATT: I didn't, you know—. I don't try to be an asshole.

MEG: No, I'm sorry. I lied.

MATT: If you're not having a baby—

MEG: About therapy.

MATT: Okay.

MEG: You asked. If I had gone, and I said no, but I did. I mean, not for a long time or anything.

MATT: How long?

MEG: Once.

(MEG *goes for the remote, but* MATT *stops her.*)

MATT: You went to therapy once? And what, that was it, all better, move on to the next thing? You're unbelievable. It's a process, you know? A process.

MEG: I only had one thing to say.

MATT: One day, Meggie, it's all going to come crashing down around you, all that speed, all that competence.

MEG: I had to tell her about the janitor.

MATT: Oh my God. Were you raped by a janitor? Is that why you're so O C D about cleanliness?

MEG: Forget it.

MATT: Tell me.

MEG: I went to the therapist in college. I was dating Jacob, and he thought I had some issues about intimacy, that I should talk to someone—

MATT: I always liked Jacob.

MEG: So I went. Once. For him. The therapist, this woman Deb, was like "what would you like to talk about?" And all I could say was "the janitor." The night Mom died, I don't know if you remember, Dad took me into the hospital cafeteria to talk about it. You were there all day and I came after school and we sat by her until she sort of fell asleep, and the doctors said she probably only had a few more hours.

MATT: I know.

MEG: And then Dad was like, "I need to talk to you, Meg," and he left you with Aunt Sharon and we went downstairs.

MATT: Yeah.

MEG: You were really young.

MATT: I remember.

MEG: Anyway, we're in the cafeteria, which is now closed and he sits me down at one of the tables and starts to talk. About how much you need me. About how my job is to take care of you now, to look after you, about how he's not sure he can make it without Mom, and the whole time, all I can focus on is the janitor. In the corner opposite us, there's this poor guy, stacking up the chairs on the tables and mopping the floor. Dad, being clueless, continues, he wants me to promise him that I'll take over for Mom and I say, "sure, yes, of course," but I'm just looking at the janitor thinking, "Dad, please, shut up. This is so embarrassing, why do we have to be having this conversation here, now? Why can't we just let this man mop the floor in peace?"

MATT: Your mother was about to—

MEG: I know.

MATT: And you were thinking about the hurt feelings of the janitor?

MEG: It was embarrassing. It was rude. And then, God, I'll never forget this, he—

MATT: Dad?

MEG: The janitor. He takes out this floor waxer, this big metal thing with a whirling disc at the bottom and he starts waxing the floor, and it makes this sound, like "vrrrrrrr", and Dad's oblivious, and so the janitor's being respectful, you know, he can tell we're having an intense conversation, so he doesn't wax near us, he just goes around in little circles on his side of the cafeteria, glancing over to see if we're done, if he can finish his job and go home to his wife, to his family. But Dad talks, vrrrrrr, and he keeps talking, vrrrrrrrr, and, finally, he stops and asks if I have any questions, and I say no, no, anything to get out of there, and we leave and go back upstairs to Mom.

MATT: What did the therapist say?

MEG: She said it sounded like I never really had time to deal with my mother's death because I was too busy focusing on the needs of others.

MATT: And you decided that's it for therapy?

MEG: More or less.

MATT: I love that I'm always the focus of the mental health interventions around here.

MEG: Anyway. I thought you should know. I don't like lying to you—

MATT: You just like not telling me things. There's a difference. It's subtle, but—

MEG: Please?

MATT: No, thanks for telling me. Really.

MEG: That's all. I didn't like her much anyway, you know. Deb. She had one of those dream catcher things in her office.

MATT: Good reason to stop.

MEG: I thought so.

MATT: You know, I was with Mom.

MEG: Huh?

MATT: When you guys went downstairs. I didn't know where you were, but, I mean, I didn't want to sit with Aunt Sharon and who knew how much time Mom had—

MEG: You went in alone?

MATT: I guess. I don't know. I think a nurse saw me go in but she didn't say anything.

MEG: You disturbed Mom? She was sleeping.

MATT: She woke up.

MEG: No she didn't. You were little, you probably got confused. The doctor said—

MATT: She woke up. I remember. She saw me there by the bed and woke up.

MEG: And you didn't tell anyone? Why didn't you go get—

MATT: I don't know. I was ten. I wasn't even supposed to be in there.

MEG: Did she look at you?

MATT: Yeah.

MEG: Did she say anything?

MATT: No. I just kind of held her hand for a while, and then she went back to sleep, and I went back out to the hall and played my Gameboy until you guys came up.

MEG: Did you talk about this with your therapist?

MATT: Nah. I mostly just talked about how much I wanted to kill you.

MEG: Thanks.

MATT: It's a joke.

MEG: Ha ha ha. You got to say goodbye to her?

MATT: I guess. A little.

MEG: I never—

MATT: I know.

MEG: She always liked you better.

MATT: Meg.

MEG: It's a joke.

MATT: Ha ha ha.

MEG: She was a guidance counselor. You needed guidance. It's fine. It doesn't bother me now.

MATT: You never needed guidance?

MEG: By the time I needed guidance, she was gone.

MATT: Would you ask her about the baby?

(Pause)

MEG: Yeah. I guess. I mean, I know what she'd say. *(Simultaneous with* MATT *below)* "Whatever makes you happy, honey."

MATT: *(Simultaneous with* MEG *above)* "Whatever makes you happy, honey."

MEG: But I would anyway.

MATT: I think she'd ask why you're not using a real man.

MEG: Matt—

MATT: I think she would. I think she would have liked a son-in-law.

MEG: Yeah, well, I would have liked a husband, but that's not the way it worked out, is it?

MATT: It's not too late—

MEG: It is for me. I've done the math—I need to get a move on. I can't just sit around waiting for someone—

MATT: You could try. I mean, I know you're my sister and everything, but you're not hideous. You could probably meet someone if—

MEG: What, if I went out more? If I dressed sexier?

MATT: If you didn't eat crap like—

MEG: This isn't crap, it's from Trader Joe's.

MATT: If you really wanted to.

MEG: This is great, I'm taking relationship advice from you. And what's your patented strategy? Meet strung-out nineteen-year-olds on the Internet?

MATT: Christy is not—

MEG: That sounds awesome. I should totally try it.

MATT: She broke up with me.

MEG: Oh. Sweetie. I'm sorry. That's awful.

MATT: It's fine.

MEG: Do you want to talk about it? I can make cocoa and—

MATT: I don't want to talk about it. At all.

MEG: Okay, but when you do—

MATT: I think Mom would want you to be in a relationship.

MEG: That makes two of us.

MATT: And not to be doing the testing tomorrow. Mom would never have—

MEG: You don't know what Mom would have said about it, they hadn't even invented genetic testing—

MATT: I know a lot better than you do. You think you're just like her, you know, with your calendars and your schedules and your color-coded folders—

MEG: A lot of people color-code.

MATT: The way you put your turn signals on like a block before you have to turn. You load a dishwasher like her.

MEG: At least I know how to—

MATT: But you're not. All those kids she talked about at school, all those fuck-ups. She loved them. She loved them more the more fucked-up they were.

MEG: It's not the same—

MATT: I don't think she'd be happy about what you're doing, and I think she'd tell you. About the sperm donor, about you having the kid alone, about the testing—

MEG: *(Overlapping)* I might be alone, but I'm going to have this kid, the embryos are already created—

MATT: About the testing.

MEG: I'm not Mom. I can't do what she did.

MATT: What's the risk of you passing it on? Statistically.

MEG: About fifteen percent, given you. And Dad.

MATT: Which is how many?

MEG: One out of seven. Therabouts.

MATT: So one of your seven embryos has it.

MEG: Statistically. Statistically, one of the seven embryos is likely to have it. Maybe more. Maybe none. No way to know for sure.

MATT: Without the testing.

MEG: Exactly.

MATT: Mom just had a kid like normal people have kids.

MEG: We don't live in that world anymore.

MATT: Think about it. You could just call up the lab and ask them not to run the bipolar test. You could.

MEG: Matt.

MATT: What would happen? You'd probably be fine.

MEG: I wouldn't know.

MATT: Mom didn't know.

MEG: But—

MATT: She would look at you like, even if she was annoyed, even if she wanted to spank you—especially when she wanted to spank you—she still loved you. That the love wasn't going to go away.

MEG: She looked at you like that. She looked at Dad.

MATT: She looked at you like that, too. She forgave you for being such a goody-two-shoes.

MEG: I don't think I was exactly a—

MATT: Don't you want to be a mom like that?

MEG: I—. Of course I do.

MATT: Because that's what she would want you to be. "All I do the whole night through is dream of you."

MEG: Seriously?

(*Pause.* MEG *looks at* MATT.)

MEG: "With the dawn I still go on dreaming of you."

MATT: "You're every thought, you're every thing"

MEG: "You're every song I'll ever sing"

MATT: Weird that her lullaby was from the scene in the movie where the hookers jump out of the cake.

MEG: They weren't hookers, they were entertainers.

MATT: They couldn't sing very well.

MEG: They were dancers.

MATT: Or hookers.

MEG: "Summer, winter, autumn and spring."

MATT: Whatever makes you happy, honey.

MEG: Matt—

MATT: Could you say that to your kid? Could you mean it?

MEG: If I didn't get the test—

MATT: Yeah?

MEG: Just the bipolar one, okay?

MATT: Okay.

MEG: It wouldn't mean I didn't want the best for the baby. Mom wanted the best for us, she did.

MATT: Sure she did. You're really, you're not going to—

MEG: I'm thinking about it. But yeah. Yeah.

Scene 6

(Inside MATT's brain. He is holding the Speak & Spell toy, now covered in knobs, re-wired, and plugged into an amplifier.)

MATT: It's impossible. What I'm trying to do now. Completely impossible. But I guess that's what makes it worthwhile, right? Meg gave me this calendar once with inspirational quotes from famous women, you ripped off a page each day. She's not—. She's not the best with gifts. Anyway, there was this Eleanor Roosevelt quote about doing six impossible things before breakfast. After that, I stopped tearing the pages off. I mean, what was the point? I was just waking up to realize yet again that Eleanor Roosevelt had beaten me. I don't even eat breakfast. Back to my point. This is impossible. This...is my brain. Pretty hot, huh? If you were comparing it with a normal brain, with Meg's brain, for example, in a scan, the first thing you'd notice is more activity. Clusters of neurons lighting up.

(White lights turn on.)

MATT: It means—oh wait, this is the really awesome part, no one knows what it means, scientists have remarked on it, studied it, documented it, but, at the end of the day, all they can tell me is: I'm different. White blobby different. Thanks for the info. The parts of my brain that are supposed to work normally, to deal with emotion and ambition, my "affective" states, in a normal brain, they work like this.

(MATT presses a button on the toy, and a sentence comes out, clear and mechanical.)

MATT: Nice, predictable. Sometimes you're happy, sometimes you're sad, but you're balanced. It's comprehensible. What some people would call "being on an even keel." Here, though, inside me, it's like this.

(MATT presses a button and the sound comes out, high and squeaky.)

MATT: Or this.

(MATT presses another and it's muddy and dense)

MATT: Or this. Or this. Or this. Or this.

(A faster and more chaotic series of distorted sounds fill the room.)

MATT: And if you don't have it, if you don't live with
this kind of brain, then you don't know.
You can't know. You think, "I am sometimes hyper
and yet sometimes lethargic. He must be like me,
except, you know, unable to get his act together. He's
lazy, selfish, probably drinks and does drugs." But
you are so completely ignorant of what it actually feels
like. How there are times when things are great, not
just great, that's a stupid word, extraordinary. You are
smart and you are focused and the paintings at the
Hirshhorn look better and ice cream tastes better and
sex is unreal and constant because when you're like
this, I have to admit, you're very attractive to women.
And things are better because you're better, better than
anyone, and you know that your life is finally on track
and things are going to be amazing, once you finish
that site you're working on and get that tattoo and buy
that new phone and call that girl and you drive like
you're flying, and maybe, yeah, maybe you do drink a
little more or smoke a little more weed, but it's worth
it because you're unstoppable. And then you're past
unstoppable and you're talking a mile a minute and
you try to call Bill Gates and Rick Rubin because you
just had the best idea ever and you need to get to the
racetracks right now because you're going to make
a million dollars and by the way you're an expert
kickboxer and you have to punch someone and fuck
someone and you just can't stop.
Until it stops. Until a few weeks or months or years
later. Until you stop, completely, and the neurons
or synapses or chemicals that were sustaining you
go kaput and suddenly you're nothing. Everything
goes gray and you sleep until noon or later because,
whatever, it doesn't matter, what the fuck point is
there in waking up anyway, it's not like you'd do
anything of worth. You're this useless blob, drain
on the resources of the planet and your family, and

everything you do just confirms everyone else's
suspicions that they've always had that you're a
pointless, fuck-up, piece of shit, and, what the hell, so
you drink a little more or smoke a little more weed, but
what else are you going to do and who's going to care
anyway—
And not all the time. Not even most of the time, things
can be good, you can have a good patch, a normal
patch, a normal couple of years, but sometimes.
Sometimes one, sometimes the other, and here, again,
the brilliant part—no one knows why. Those doctors,
they can tell you what you have, they can even tell
you what to take—four hundred and fifty milligrams
of Lithium twice a day—to keep it calm, prevent the
episodes of mania, the periods of depression, but no
one knows exactly why, how the chemicals work,
which bolts of electricity do what. It's been going on
for thousands of years, and everyone's still like, "Um, I
don't know. Pill?"
Hippocrates first described bipolar disorder, it was
one of the first diseases to be described, did you know
that? He called it melancholia—caused by an excess
of black bile from the spleen—but the symptoms were
pretty much the same: periods of glee, periods of
sadness. Meg showed me, she found this ancient Greek
medical textbook in the library—she loves context—
and Hippocrates describes this woman. From Thasos?
Or whatever. Somewhere Greek. She couldn't sleep,
she couldn't eat, she would curse at people and freak
out and have to be restrained, but she was also, like,
sad and morose because of, in Hippocrates's words,
a "justifiable grief." Her feelings were justifiable, but,
her actions? Oh no, that's out of control, that needs to
be restrained, that's upsetting to people. That's nuts.
That—all of it, every part that I wouldn't trade for
anything—that's me.

Scene 7

(MEG *is thinking about it.* MATT *enters holding his computer and a mug of cocoa, elaborately decorated with whipped cream.*)

MATT: For you. Cocoa.

(MATT *hands* MEG *the mug.*)

MEG: Thanks. (*She takes a sip.*) What's in here? It's good. It's—

MATT: Cinnamon. Cayenne pepper. Some other stuff, I kind of just raided the fridge.

MEG: Did you use my immersion blender?

MATT: Does it taste good?

MEG: Yeah. Thanks.

MATT: I made something else. I want you to take a look at it, okay?

MEG: Okay.

MATT: And you're still thinking of not—

MEG: Yes.

MATT: Really?

MEG: Yes. I'm really thinking about it.

MATT: Because I think this might help.

MEG: So the cocoa's to butter me up?

MATT: Just look.

MEG: Honestly, I have been thinking about Mom, and what you said, and taking chances, and I do want to be that kind of parent, accepting and—

MATT: All right, check it out. It's a—. I started it a couple weeks ago, I wanted to move into a different direction, you know, take more charge of myself and what I'm making. It's, um, it's like an interactive digital media installation, inspired by the work of Toshio Iwai, along the lines of Electroplankton.

MEG: Okay.

MATT: It's on my laptop.

MEG: Like a website?

MATT: Well, except that—. Yeah, you know what, sure, like a website.

MEG: Give it.

(MATT *hands* MEG *the computer.*)

MATT: You start here, at this portal, and then, you can navigate through, like whatever direction you want. But, see, your actions will also determine the interface elements—

(*Music and lights start flashing from the screen.*)

MATT: And then, okay, if you go that way, there are situations, stimuli, things to respond to.

MEG: Like a video game?

MATT: No, I mean, I guess a little, but there's nothing to win or lose, you know, just to, like, interact with—

MEG: What do I do now?

MATT: What do you want to do?

MEG: You tell me. You made it, which door?

MATT: Portal.

MEG: So it is a video game.

MATT: Forget it.

MEG: Come on. Tell me.

MATT: Well, it's supposed to be up to you, you know, that you're the one creating your own environment, instead of just moving through some pre-programmed set of—ooh, open that.

MEG: What?

MATT: Click on it. It's gonna disappear soon, so you have to click on—

MEG: What? Click on what?

MATT: The spark. In the corner.

MEG: Here?

(MEG *clicks on something. The computer starts to make strange sounds.*)

MATT: Shit. Shit. Shit. Shit.

MEG: Did I do something wrong? I tried to click on the—

(MATT *tries to quit the computer program but it's not responding.*)

MATT: Come on, you little piece of crap program. Force quit, motherfucker.

MEG: I thought I was pressing the spark, I mean, there were a lot of sparks, but I thought I—

MATT: Reboot. What, you won't even reboot now?

MEG: I bet—

MATT: Could you just shut up for a second?

MEG: Okay.

(*Pause*)

MEG: You know, I'm sure you can fix it, it's probably nothing.

MATT: It's not nothing! I've been working on this for, like, weeks and it's really complex and I brought it out here to show you that I'm not just a lunatic, I'm also creative, that it's not so bad, it's just different, okay, but this stupid fucking computer—

(MATT *is about to throw the computer.*)

MEG: Calm down. Okay? Okay?

(MEG *tries to soothe* MATT. *He bats her hand away.*)

MATT: Stop it! How could it just shut down? Why won't it reboot again, what did you do to it? This program, this installation, is really important, it's going to be a really, really big deal. It's my thing, it's going to be the thing that—

MEG: Mattie, you need to calm down.

(MEG *holds* MATT*'s shoulders. She takes the computer and puts it down.*)

MATT: It's just—. You don't even understand, you don't—

MEG: Shhhhhhh.

(MEG *takes his head and puts it in her lap. She pats his hair. This is a very familiar posture for both of them.*)

MEG: Shhhhh. It's okay. It's going to be okay. Breathe.

(MATT *sits up*)

MATT: I can't—

MEG: Breathe.

(MATT *lies back down again. He breathes.*)

MEG: Good. Again. Good. Everything is going to be fine. I'm sure it is.

(MATT *breathes*)

MEG: You made all that?

MATT: Uh huh.

MEG: All the graphics and the colors and—

MATT: Yeah.

MEG: And the music, did you—

MATT: I mean, I found some shit on-line and fucked with it, you know?

MEG: No. But, I mean, it was really impressive. If, and I don't know if you want to, but if you ever wanted to apply to school again, this would make a great—

MATT: You didn't recognize it?

MEG: Was I supposed to?

MATT: Never mind.

MEG: It sounded interesting. You're good at stuff like that.

MATT: Until it breaks.

MEG: You can fix it. Right?

MATT: Probably.

MEG: See?

MATT: Thanks. I'm glad you like it. I've been working on it a lot.

MEG: I can tell.

MATT: Because this is the kind of stuff I want to do, you know. Not just make shit for other people. God, do you know what the graphic design jobs in D C are like? It's all, like, white columns, and eagles, and gold scrolls and shit. You know how many people want their website to contain Flash of a fucking billowing flag?

(Pause)

MEG: Matt, honey—

MATT: What?

(MEG *breathes in, holds it, and then breathes out.*)

MATT: What? What?

MEG: Did you—. Have you been taking your medication?

(MATT *moves off the couch.*)

MATT: Fuck you.

MEG: I'm sorry—. You're acting really...intense. And I'm wondering if maybe—. You said you weren't sleeping—

MATT: Because I've been working on this, like I said—

MEG: I know, but it's—. Last time when you skipped a couple days—

MATT: Do you trust me?

MEG: Of course I do.

MATT: Then you should trust that I took it.

MEG: Did you?

MATT: You don't.

MEG: I do. I just want to know—. I'm worried, you seem really high-energy. Volatile.

MATT: I wonder why. I wonder what you might be doing tomorrow in a lab with some embryos that might make me tense.

MEG: Don't do this. Don't blame me for—

MATT: You're just a tease.

MEG: What?

MATT: You are. That's what you do. You act like you're going to listen to me, but really it's just a ploy to—

MEG: I'm glad you showed the computer thing to me, Matt. Really. It's good. It's exciting when you make things, I like it. I just worry about the fact that it's really late and you're bouncing off the walls, and I'm afraid it's a sign of—

MATT: I think you're jealous.

MEG: I'm—

MATT: I think you're jealous of me, and that's why you wanted to do the testing, so you won't be jealous of your kid.

MEG: Jealous? Are you kidding?

MATT: Do you know how many great artists were bipolar?

MEG: Okay, look—

MATT: I bet you never thought of that when you were handing out gold stars to the best fetuses—

MEG: That's just—. First of all, it's not a fetus, and—

MATT: But you're going to.

MEG: Can you not bring this up right now? We were talking about you and your medication.

MATT: Are you going to call the lab tomorrow and cancel the testing? Are you?

MEG: I—. I don't know.

MATT: All you can see is the bad stuff. You're so afraid of something going wrong that you can't even imagine the possibility that one of those substandard babies—

MEG: Stop, Matt, please. I am thinking about it, really, but it's hard when you—

MATT: It might be a genius.

MEG: Interrupt me as I'm thinking.

MATT: Can you admit it? Can you admit that these, what, cell clumps, all right, fine, make it sound like something that clogs your shower drain, but these cell clumps have real possibility. Maybe genius possibility. Did you think about that? Did you?

MEG: I can't talk to you when you're like this.

MATT: You can talk to me. You're talking to me right
now. But you're not listening. Not to the fact that even
if this eight-cell blob can't be proven to be a person, if it
screens positive for the bipolar gene, which probably,
one of them will, right? Right?

MEG: Statistically.

MATT: Statistically one of them will, so there's a chance,
like a very good chance that this, this cell clump might
grow up to be the next Byron or Van Gogh or Sylvia
Plath or—

MEG: Or probably it won't.

MATT: You are jealous.

MEG: I am not a genius, Matt, okay, and I don't need to
produce one. I just want my child to be happy.

MATT: To be boring.

MEG: To be happy.

MATT: Like you are?

(Pause)

MEG: You're right. I am jealous. Jealous of how selfish
you get to be.

MATT: I'm selfish?

MEG: All day long, while you work, while you hang
out, while you jerk off, while you make your projects,
you're thinking about you.

MATT: You have no idea, you don't even look at—

MEG: "What's my new idea? I'm so excited. I'm so
depressed." And for me, all day long, at work, at home,
do you know what I'm thinking about? I'm thinking
about you.

MATT: I never asked you to think about me. Maybe
Dad did, but I—

MEG: I don't have a choice. You have the indescribable luxury of being able to concentrate on your emotions, you spend hours wallowing in their ups and downs—

MATT: It's not like that—

MEG: So you ask me if I'm happy, Matt, well guess what? I don't know. It's not something I give a lot of attention.

MATT: I don't know when you decided you needed to be my parent, but this wasn't my idea. And I didn't ask you to live like this, you asked me to leave Bloomington and come here, remember?

MEG: The baby makes me happy. The idea of this baby makes me happy, something small and soft and new. And happy.

MATT: So, fine, take your perfect, problem-free baby, install her in my bedroom and kick me to the curb.

MEG: I would never kick you—

MATT: But I'm not going to keep living here am I? Once it's born?

MEG: We don't need to have that conversation now.

MATT: Well, when are we going to have it?

MEG: It's late, we're both tired. You're apparently starting a medication holiday.

MATT: Off topic.

MEG: I don't think—. I don't think it makes sense for us to talk about living situations or whatever in this condition. In the morning, when you're calmer, when we're both calmer, we can look at the options—

MATT: And what are "the options", Meg?

MEG: Well, I think, for one, we both have always known that this situation was temporary.

MATT: Uh huh.

MEG: Just, mathematically, it's a two-bedroom apartment. We're going to be three people.

MATT: So you are kicking me out. I knew you would do that, I knew couldn't trust—

MEG: I am not kicking you out, that is so unfair. You can stay here as long as you need to find somewhere new. I mean, the baby can be in my room for the first couple of months if it has to be—

MATT: And then what?

MEG: And then we can find you a place nearby, somewhere really cute, like in Adams Morgan or Mount Pleasant, a group house or a place of your own—

MATT: Like a halfway house?

MEG: That's not what I mean.

MATT: We had a deal.

MEG: It wasn't a permanent deal. It's been years—

MATT: Forget it. And, look, if you don't want to think about me all day, just fucking stop. I certainly don't spend my free time thinking about you.

MEG: I'd noticed.

MATT: I mean it. God, you're so obsessed with your own responsibility—perfect daughter, perfect sister, perfect mom. But what if we didn't need you, huh? What would happen to Meg then? Maybe she'd evaporate. Or go insane.

MEG: You don't need me.

MATT: Maybe I don't. Maybe I'd be better off if you never tried to rescue me. Maybe I'd have a job and a car and girlfriend and a goldfish and be stable just like you want if you had left me the hell alone.

MEG: Matt?

MATT: What?

MEG: You'd be dead.

MATT: Bullshit.

MEG: I'm sorry. It's true. You crashed your car—

MATT: It was an accident.

MEG: Into a tree. On an empty road. I don't think that was accidental. Neither did the doctors.

MATT: Well, I do. Anyway, you weren't there, were you? Were you?

MEG: Give me your wallet.

MATT: Why?

MEG: I mean it. Give it.

MATT: There's no money—

MEG: That's a surprise. When I came back home to Bloomington and saw you after the crash, the doctors said to be careful, and I said it'd be okay. That you'd be good, now that there was a diagnosis and you could get treatment. We'd figure out a way to make it work.

(MATT *hands* MEG *his wallet.*)

MEG: But just in case. Here. See this? (*She takes out a piece of paper.*)

MEG: In case of emergency, please call Meg O'Reilly.

MATT: So?

MEG: So that's our relationship. I am your emergency contact. You're your own emergency.

MATT: Who's your emergency contact?

MEG: I don't have one.

MATT: And if something happened to you?

MEG: It won't. I'm not the one things happen to. You are.

(MEG *hands* MATT *back his wallet.*)

MATT: You want me gone.

MEG: No. Not any time soon. I want you to stay and be okay, and you'll get back on your medication and I'll keep my doctor's appointments and we'll all be healthy and safe.

MATT: No, you'll be healthy and safe and your baby will be healthy and safe and I'll be the big, dead-weight emotional crabgrass that you're trying to weed out of your life.

MEG: Just get some rest—

(MATT *goes to the computer and starts to play the music from the program.*)

MATT: You really didn't recognize it?

(*The music is a distorted, propulsive version of the song* Singin' in the Rain.)

MATT: I try to make something, and you can't even see it for what it is. (*He begins to dance a spastic tap-dance around the room.*)

MEG: Watch it, be careful.

(MATT *picks up a makeshift umbrella and begins jumping on piles of* MEG's *papers as if they were puddles.*)

MATT: You can't even see me when I'm right in front of you.

MEG: Stop it.

(MATT *goes into his big finish. The music stops.*)

MEG: I see you. I do. And I'm worried.

(MATT *throws the laptop at* MEG.)

MATT: Catch.

(MEG *catches it.*)

MEG: If you don't want me to have the tests, try taking your goddamn medication.

MATT: Why?

MEG: Show me that a person with this disease can live a normal, functioning life.

MATT: Like you do? You said you were going to think about it.

(MATT *exits to his room, leaving* MEG *holding the laptop.*)

MEG: I am Matt. I am thinking about it.

Scene 8

(MEG *is banging on* MATT's *door. He's been in there for a while.*)

MEG: Matt, come on out of there. Please—what are you doing? I'm getting worried. Matt.

(MATT *enters carrying a realistic-looking homemade fetus puppet.*)

MATT: I made it. See? Just now, for you.

(MEG *is speechless.*)

MATT: Hi Meg! I'm your embryo. Don't screen me, all I want to do is DANCE!

(MATT *enacts a short vaudeville routine on the couch with the puppet, humming* Make 'Em Laugh, *then brings it in to kiss* MEG.)

MEG: Get that away from me! (*She swats at it.*)

MATT: Baby killer. Don't worry, honey, she didn't mean it.

MEG: Matt!

MATT: Joke. It's a joke. I don't see why—. I'm just trying to have a sense of humor about this whole thing, okay? God.

MEG: It's sick. It's disgusting.

MATT: It's a little funny.

MEG: It's not funny.

MATT: I think it's funny. I think lots of people would think that it's funny. Lots and lots and lots of—

MEG: Just tell me, how long have you been off your medication? A day? Two days?

MATT: For real?

MEG: Just tell me. I won't get mad.

MATT: A couple weeks.

MEG: Weeks? You've never—

MATT: Four weeks. A month. That night when you told me you were going to have a baby, I stopped—

MEG: Matt. That's way too long, you're in really fragile territory—

MATT: No. Listen, how I feel on lithium compared to how I feel now, it's like being underwater, it's like having wax buildup in your brain, and then, going off it, it's like a giant Q-Tip comes and scours you and finally you're clean, you know? It's like, it's like, it's like I'm blurry when I'm on meds, and I don't make things—

MEG: When you're not on your meds, you're not sane.

MATT: Maybe I don't want to be sane. Maybe saneness is overrated, and where I am right now, that's reality. Or better than reality.

MEG: Is this why Christy broke up with you?

MATT: Fuck off.

MEG: I won't. Go to the bathroom and take your pill.

MATT: I don't want to.

MEG: I don't care if you want to, you need to. This is serious.

MATT: What does it matter?

MEG: What else have you been up to? Are you gambling? Matt—

MATT: So? What if I am? You can pay my bills right?

MEG: From your trust. It's not infinite, and I thought you were saving it for college. If you want to blow it all while you're becoming manic, be my guest but—

MATT: Trust. Isn't that hysterical, that they call it a trust, because, clearly, if someone establishes one for you, if you happen to have the money left over from selling your parents' house in trust, well then the one thing that is clear is that you are not trusted. It's almost like someone thought, "hey, I know, if we call it a trust, they won't notice the complete and utter lack of trust involved." It's like the way they call shitty buildings for storing old, decrepit people homes. Like "don't worry, Grampa, we're putting you in a home." Never mind that you're actually taking him out of his home, I guess they think, "if we call it a home, everyone will be fooled."

MEG: Could you sit down? Just take a seat. I want you to do that and then I'm going to get your pills—

MATT: What happens to the rejects? (*He starts to move the puppet again in a slow dance.*)

MEG: What do you mean?

MATT: You know, after the testing, some lucky embryos will advance to the next round, which is an all-expense paid trip to your uterus, but what happens to the poor suckers unlucky enough not to make it?

MEG: You really want to know? Will you take your pills if I tell you?

MATT: Yeah. I will.

MEG: Well, there are lots of options. You can freeze them for future use, if you want, or give them to another woman. You ought to be able to donate them to scientific research as stem cells—

MATT: Or. Or.

MEG: Or they could be discarded.

MATT: Thrown out.

MEG: Yeah.

MATT: If they're defective and diseased and nobody wants them?

MEG: It's not—

MATT: In the trash?

MEG: I don't know. I guess. I guess that's where they'd go, if they went—

(MATT *screams in his fetus voice and tosses the puppet in the trashcan.*)

MATT: Like that?

MEG: It doesn't look like that. It's just eight cells. You couldn't even see it with your naked eye. I've been trying to tell you, it's not a person.

MATT: Then why did you freak out about my puppet?

MEG: Because you always do this.

MATT: Actually, it's my first. I'm quite proud of how it came out.

MEG: Matt. This. Whenever I'm on the verge of something, you flare up, and suddenly I'm in triage mode, on what's supposed to be the happiest day of my life—

MATT: That's your wedding.

MEG: Well, for me, it's—

MATT: You wish I had never been born. That's why you're eradicating me.

MEG: I've told you, this has nothing to do with you. I'm not doing anything to you.

MATT: That's why you want me on lithium. You only like me when I'm acting like somebody else.

MEG: You're yourself on meds, you're your best self.

MATT: I'm the easiest to deal with.

MEG: Jesus, you are being so unfair right now.

MATT: And you are trying to delete me from our family. You are genetically editing me from the code of who we are. You're eliminating me and you're eliminating Dad.

MEG: Dad has nothing to do with this.

MATT: Dad has everything to do with this. You don't want me to end up like him, you don't want this kid to end up like him—

MEG: No, all right, I don't—

MATT: I found him. You went away to go to your fancy college, and I found him after class. He had stopped eating, bathing, he just sat in the dark all day in the house with those cats—he got these fucking cats after you left—

MEG: I remember—

MATT: He was reading the same books over and over again. He was supposedly on sabbatical, but really he was just in the dark.

MEG: It's not your fault—

MATT: I didn't even know he had a gun. I mean, Dad? With a gun? He had a little instruction manual. He had to use an instruction manual.

MEG: I know how you feel.

MATT: You don't! I was there. And I couldn't stop it. I couldn't prevent him—I couldn't fix Mom and I couldn't help Dad, and I'm not going to let another one go, I'm not going to let you get rid of another member of our family—

MEG: Mattie, it's not the same thing. No one's blaming you for their deaths. It sounds like you have a lot you want to talk about, which is great, and you should talk about it, but for now, you need to—

MATT: If you wanted a baby so much, why didn't you have one with your stupid boyfriend? Because he got sick of you, so now you're alone and you're trying to destroy me.

MEG: Jacob didn't get sick of me. He got sick of you.

MATT: What are you talking about?

MEG: Jacob broke up with me after I brought you back here from Bloomington. He said that he wanted to date me—to move in with me—not me and my bipolar brother.

MATT: No. Stop lying to me. No! No! No!

MEG: Come on, why don't you come sit on the couch? Put your head in my—

(MEG *goes to* MATT *to lead him to the couch.*)

MATT: I could put a baby in you. I could put all the bipolar genes in my body in yours right now and you'd have the most messed up kid imaginable—

MEG: Shhh, Mattie. You don't mean that. You're not yourself.

(MATT *hits* MEG, *hard. She falls to the floor.*)

MATT: Shit, shit, shit. I'm sorry, I'm such a fucking disaster. Are you okay?

MEG: Don't touch me.

MATT: Meg, listen, you gotta understand, ever since I went off the lithium, all I've been thinking about is it, this kid, I wanna be there for it—

MEG: You have to leave. I can't have you around like this, not when there's going to be a baby. If I'd been pregnant—

MATT: Who's going to show her what stars look like, or that crayons draw better on walls, she needs someone who can tell her that it's okay to be little crazy sometimes, that you can make up your own songs if you want to, and I can be that person, I mean, I can be a really fucking kick-ass uncle, I think, only—. I want to be there for her, you know, whoever she is and whatever she wants. I want to love that baby the way you can't.

MEG: Get out. Get out of here.

(MEG *throws* MATT's *jacket at him. He leaves.*)

MEG: I'm calling your doctor!

Scene 9

(*Back in* MEG's *womb. Six weeks later*)

MEG: The piece of paper, with my phone number. It's still in his wallet—I think—so the fact that I haven't heard anything for the past six weeks, that he hasn't called. That the police haven't called. The hospitals. I'm trying to take it as good news.
I got the tests. The next day. I thought about it, calling up to cancel, saying "just implant whatever embryos

you want, let's take a risk" but I couldn't do it. I
couldn't handle the thought, the guilt of saying to a
child "I could have prevented your feeling this way,
but I chose not to."Adrianna said there were several
top-quality embryos, disease-free, healthy and plump,
and since often one doesn't take, that I should consider
transferring two. So, to be on the safe side, I did.
Impregnation by appointment—I never quite pictured
it happening in one of those paper gowns, but it wasn't
so bad, all things considered. She was very gentle. And
then, unexpectedly, they both implanted. They popped
up on the ultrasound at my next appointment—two
little heartbeats. My twin daughters. I had asked for
girls, of course, but, today, when I got my paperwork
in the mail, I saw instead: the two embryos were
labeled XX and XY. I couldn't believe it, I figured it
was a typo, so I called just to make sure. And they
checked—not a typo. It turns out someone at the lab
had made a mistake, implanted one of the other top-
quality disease-free embryos. It happens sometimes.
They were very apologetic, but, you know. Human
error.

And here we are again. In my womb. Looks different,
doesn't it? Hunkering down for the next seven and
a half months of gestation. Cozier. Fuller. Kind of
like a cave for hibernating, or at least, that's how I'm
thinking of it. A resting place for my two little bears.
That over there, behind you is Katherine. I'm thinking
Katie. This one—

(*The actor playing* MATT *enters in a perfect Gene Kelly
costume and begins to dance—flawlessly.*)

MEG: This is Matt.

END OF PLAY